EDGE BOOKS™

Foxhounds, Coonhounds, and Other

HOUND DOGS

by Tammy Gagne

CAPSTONE PRESS
a capstone imprint

Edge Books are published by Capstone Press,
1710 Roe Crest Drive, North Mankato, Minnesota 56003
www.mycapstone.com

Library of Congress Cataloging-in-Publication Data
Names: Gagne, Tammy, author.
Title: Foxhounds, Coonhounds, and other hound dogs / by Tammy Gagne.
Description: North Mankato, Minnesota : Capstone Press, [2017] | Series: Dog
   encyclopedias | Audience: Ages 9-12. | Audience: Grades 4 to 6. |
   Includes bibliographical references and index.
Summary: Informative text and vivid photos introduce readers to various
   hound dog breeds.
Identifiers: LCCN 2015043103 (print) | LCCN 2015046140 (ebook) |
   ISBN 978-1-5157-0302-0 (library binding) | ISBN 978-1-5157-0310-5 (ebook pdf)
Subjects: LCSH: Hounds—Juvenile literature. | Dog breeds—Juvenile
   literature.
Classification: LCC SF429.H6 G34 2017 (print) | LCC SF429.H6 (ebook) |
   DDC 636.753—dc23
LC record available at http://lccn.loc.gov/2015043103

Editorial Credits
Alesha Halvorson, editor; Terri Poburka, designer; Kelly Garvin, media researcher;
Katy LaVigne, production specialist

Photo Credits
Alamy/John Cancalosi, 14 (top); Getty Images/Neilson Barnard/USA Network/NBCU Photo Bank, 7 (t); Newscom: Dorling Kindersley/Universal Images Group, 7 (bottom), 14 (b), 17 (b), 21 (b), 23 (b); Shutterstock: ARTSILENSE, 6 (b), Capture Light, 16 (t), cyanoclub, 28 (b), DragoNika, 6 (t), 20 (t), 27 (t), eAlisa, 8 (t), Eric Isselee, 20 (b), 25 (b), 26 (b), 27 (b), Erik Lam, 13 (b), gbarinov, backcover, 11 (b), Grisha Bruev, 15 (t), Igor Normann, cover (top right), 4-5, Jagodka, 15 (b), 16 (b), 18 (b), Lenkadan, 1, 13 (t), 22 (t), Lindsay Helms, 29 (b), Misti Hymas, 8 (b), Nick Hayes, cover (bottom right), Paul Cotney, cover (left), Pelevinia Ksinia, 24 (b), Purino, 23 (t), Rita Kochmarjova, 10 (t), Robynrg, 29 (t), Rowena, 25 (t), Sally Wallis, 19 (t), siloto, 11 (t), Steve Lovegrove, 26 (t), Tatiana Katsai, 24 (t), terekhov Igor, 17 (t), tsik, 18 (t), Vivienstock, 9 (b), 28 (t), volofin 9 (t), WilleeCole Photography, 12, 22 (b), www.BillionPhoto, 10 (b); Superstock: Jean-Michel Labat/ardea.com/Panth/Pantheon, 19 (b), John Daniels/ardea.com/Panth/Pantheon, 21 (t)

Printed and bound in the United States of America.
009676F16

Table of Contents

Hunting Hounds

The American Kennel Club's (AKC) hound group is made up of 29 dog breeds. Most dogs in the hound group were developed to work as hunting dogs. Scent hounds help hunters by locating prey with their noses. These dogs have a highly developed sense of smell that is even more sensitive than that of other dog breeds. Sighthounds, also called gazehounds, rely on their sharp eyesight and wide range of vision to locate prey.

Hounds vary in their personalities as much as they do in their appearances. Some are too loud to keep in apartments or with close by neighbors. Many hounds bark or howl frequently. Many are extremely athletic, while some are couch potatoes. Some are even both active and lazy—depending on the time of day. Some make excellent pets. Others prefer to spend their time in the field.

Whether they are working dogs or companions, hounds almost always have a desire to hunt. For this reason, fenced yards and leashes are important for keeping them safe. Although these dogs share the urge to hunt, they all have something special to offer dog lovers. Get ready for an up-close look at each hound breed!

FUN FACT

The AKC is sometimes called a club of clubs. Nearly all dog breeds have their own breed clubs. Instead of covering all breeds, breed clubs focus on just one in particular.

Afghan Hound

Appearance:
Height: 24 to 29 inches (61 to 74 centimeters)
Weight: 50 to 60 pounds (23 to 27 kilograms)

With its large body and long, silky hair, the Afghan Hound is an elegant breed. These dogs have long, narrow heads that help when hunting. They can see things both in front of them and far to each side.

Personality: Afghans are athletic dogs that love their human families. Fenced yards are a smart idea for this breed because they are sighthounds. An Afghan won't just notice a squirrel—it will chase it down.

Breed Background: One of the oldest dog breeds, the Afghan Hound was developed to hunt gazelle, deer, and even leopards.

Countries of Origin:
Afghanistan, Iran, Pakistan

Recognized by AKC: 1926

Training Notes: While Afghan Hounds are smart, they are also sensitive. They respond well to patience and lots of praise.

Care Notes: Afghans need a lot of exercise. They love to run in a large, fenced area or be taken on daily walks. These dogs need their long coats brushed and washed weekly.

American English Coonhound

Appearance:
Height: 23 to 26 inches (58 to 66 cm)
Weight: 40 to 65 pounds (18 to 29 kg)

The American English Coonhound has a short coat that comes in many colors. This dog may be blue and white, red and white, or black and white. Some dogs also have **ticking**. This pattern of spots is found on the white part of the animal's coat.

Personality: American English Coonhounds are confident yet friendly with both people and other dogs. They also love kids, making these dogs great family companions.

Country of Origin: United States

Recognized by AKC: 2011

Training Notes: These intelligent dogs love pleasing their owners. However, this breed can become easily distracted and may require extra patience to train. American English Coonhounds respond well to gentle, positive training.

Care Notes: This active breed needs lots of exercise. Instead of a daily walk, American English Coonhounds should go on daily runs. Their short coats need only occasional brushing and bathing.

FUN FACT
Some people call this breed the Redtick Coonhound.

American Foxhound

Appearance:
Height: 23 to 28 inches (58 to 71 cm)
Weight: 65 to 75 pounds (29 to 34 kg)

The American Foxhound has a rough coat that protects the dog from branches and sticks when hunting in the field. Medium in length, the hair comes in many colors. The most popular combination is black, white, and tan.

Personality: This easygoing dog makes a great pet for active families. They love to tag along for hikes or jogs. American Foxhounds may not be the best choice for people with nearby neighbors though. These dogs are known for their tendency to howl loudly. This sound is called baying.

Country of Origin: United States

Recognized by AKC: 1886

Training Notes: This breed can be both stubborn and independent. Training can be challenging because American Foxhounds have a strong desire to hunt. Owners should beg training at a young age and use p praise and rewards.

Care Notes: American Foxhou need between one and two hours exercise daily. Because these dog very little, only occasional brush is needed.

Basenji

Appearance:

Height: 15 to 17 inches (38 to 43 cm)
Weight: 20 to 26 pounds (9 to 12 kg)

This short-haired breed has several features that make it easy to recognize. First, people usually notice the dog's tightly curled tail. The breed also has a wrinkled forehead and large, pointed ears.

Personality: The Basenji's voice box is shaped differently than that of other breeds. For this reason Basenjis can't bark like other dogs. Instead they make a whining sound.

Breed Background: The Basenji was and is still used to hunt lions in Africa.

Country of Origin: Congo

Recognized by AKC: 1943

Training Notes: These intelligent dogs are extremely independent, so training takes time and effort. Early **obedience** training is important for Basenjis. **Socialization** at a young age is also a good idea.

Care Notes: Basenjis are known for getting into trouble when the opportunity arises. Owners who leave their belongings out may find them chewed up. Keeping a Basenji busy with plenty of exercise may help with its chewing habits. These dogs also need occasional bathing and brushing to keep them looking their best.

FUN FACT

Some hounds hunt with their noses. Others rely on their eyes. The Basenji uses both sight and scent in the field.

Basset Hound

Appearance:
Height: 11 to 15 inches (28 to 38 cm)
Weight: 45 to 65 pounds (20 to 29 kg)

The Basset Hound has a heavy body, short legs, and the longest ears of any dog breed. Many people think this breed has a sad expression because of the animal's droopy eyes.

Personality: Bassets are affectionate and loyal dogs. They especially love spending time with children. Kids must be taught to treat these dogs with respect, however. Playing too rough with this breed can injure its long back.

Breed Background: Basset Hounds were developed by breeding Bloodhounds down to a smaller size.

Countries of Origin: France, Great Britain

Recognized by AKC: 1935

Training Notes: Basset Hounds are stubborn dogs but easy to train. These dogs have a strong urge to hunt prey, so training should begin at the puppy stage.

Care Notes: Because Basset Hounds are more likely to become **obese** than other breeds, daily exercise, including walks, is necessary. Weekly grooming, such as brushing the coat, is recommended. Owners must also clean their Basset Hounds' long ears frequently to prevent infection.

FUN FACT

Breeders who developed the Basset Hound chose dogs with white on their tails. The bright tip helped hunters spot the dogs even if they were in high brush.

Beagle

Appearance:
Height: 13 to 15 inches (33 to 38 cm)
Weight: 20 to 25 pounds (9 to 11 kg)

Beagles can be almost any color. By far the most popular variety is the **tricolor**. This combination is made up of a black **saddle**, tan head and middle, and white everywhere else.

Personality: Beagles are one of the most popular pets. They are friendly with their owners and most strangers. Beagles have a loud bark though.

Country of Origin: United Kingdom

Recognized by AKC: 1885

Training Notes: Beagles are smart dogs. Non-hunting Beagles must be kept on leashes or in fenced yards outdoors, however. These determined animals will follow any scent that tempts them. Because of their independent personality, short training sessions may work best with Beagles.

Care Notes: Beagles are playful and need a fair amount of exercise each week. Despite their short coats, Beagles need frequent baths. If anything smelly is nearby, this breed will surely roll in it. Weekly brushing is also important for these shedders.

FUN FACT

Beagles have a special sound they make when hunting. They use it to let the hunter know they are following the scent of the prey.

FAMOUS DOGS

The *Peanuts* cartoon character Snoopy is a Beagle.

Black and Tan Coonhound

Appearance:

Height: 23 to 27 inches (58 to 69 cm)
Weight: 50 to 75 pounds (23 to 34 kg)

The Black and Tan Coonhound has a short, black coat. Tan markings are found on the dog's chest, legs, and **muzzle**.

Personality: Black and Tan Coonhounds are loyal and loving dogs. They can also be protective of their owners. They may be slow to warm up to new people and other dogs.

Country of Origin: United States

Recognized by AKC: 1945

Training Notes: These intelligent dogs are quick to follow their owners anywhere. In both hunting and obedience training, a Black and Tan Coonhound has a strong desire to please its owner. Early socialization training may help these dogs warm up to strangers and other animals.

Care Notes: Black and Tan Coonhounds need daily exercise, either on a leash or in a fenced area. Frequent **currying** or brushing will keep these dogs looking their best.

Bloodhound

Appearance:
Height: 24 to 26 inches (61 to 66 cm)
Weight: 80 to 90 pounds (36 to 41 kg)

Bloodhounds have sturdy bodies, long ears, and lots of wrinkles. The breed's short, thin coat comes in several colors. Red is one of the most common coat colors for this dog.

Personality: A Bloodhound can make a wonderful pet. People considering this breed should know how much Bloodhounds drool—a lot!

Breed Background: Some people think that the Bloodhound got its name from its ability to smell blood. Bloodhounds have the most powerful noses of any dog breed. They actually got their name from their pure bloodlines.

Countries of Origin: Belgium, England, France, Scotland

Recognized by AKC: 1885

Training Notes: Owners can train Bloodhounds to do almost anything—except not follow their noses. Obedience training should begin during the puppy stage for these dogs.

Care Notes: Bloodhounds need lots of daily exercise to prevent boredom. These dogs should be brushed and bathed weekly to help them look and smell their best.

FUN FACT
A Bloodhound in Kansas once tracked a scent for 135 miles (217 km)!

FAMOUS DOGS
McGruff the Crime Dog is a Bloodhound.

Bluetick Coonhound

Appearance:

Height: 20 to 27 inches (51 to 69 cm)
Weight: 45 to 80 pounds (20 to 36 kg)

The Bluetick Coonhound's long ears and droopy eyes are the first things people notice about this breed. These short-coated dogs are either blue ticked or blue ticked and tan. The breed's name comes from both the ticking in the dog's coat and the animals it hunts—raccoons.

Personality: Bluetick Coonhounds are playful to the point of being goofy. They love to run around and make noise. For this reason they do best in homes with big backyards and no nearby neighbors.

Breed Background: The Bluetick Coonhound was developed in Louisiana. Its ancestors include the Bleu de Gascogne and the English Foxhound.

Country of Origin: United States

Recognized by AKC: 2009

Training Notes: Blueticks are smart dogs. But owners must be patient and **persistent** when training this breed. Blueticks excel at many dog sports, such as **agility**, tracking, and water races.

Care Notes: These dogs need a lot of exercise. They also enjoy being part of family activities and outdoor outings. A Bluetick's short coat should be brushed weekly.

Borzoi

Appearance:

Height: 26 to 28 inches (66 to 71 cm)
Weight: 60 to 105 pounds (27 to 48 kg)

Borzois are large dogs. Their long, silky coats can be flat, curly, or in-between. There are 18 color variations for this athletic breed.

Personality: The Borzoi is known for its incredible speed and endurance. As active as they are, these dogs love spending time with their owners. Dog enthusiasts say the Borzoi is among the most loving and gentle dog breeds.

Breed Background: The Borzoi was developed by crossing Arabian Greyhounds with sheepdogs.

Countries of Origin: Belarus, Russia

Recognized by AKC: 1891

Training Notes: Borzois need extra time and patience when training. They are naturally stubborn. Using praise and rewards, such as treats, may help a Borzoi warm up to obedience training.

Care Notes: Similar to other sighthounds, the Borzoi cannot be trusted off its leash in public. A high, fenced yard is ideal for daily running and exercise. This breed's long coat should be brushed regularly to keep it shiny and **mat**-free.

FUN FACT

The Borzoi is also known as the Russian Wolfhound. The word "borzii" is Russian for "swift."

Dachshund

Appearance:

Standard
Height: over 8 inches (20 cm)
Weight: 16 to 32 pounds (7 to 15 kg)

Miniature
Height: up to 8 inches (20 cm)
Weight: up to 11 pounds (5 kg)

Dachshunds are long dogs that stand low to the ground. Their coats can be smooth, wire-haired, or long-haired. These dogs come in two sizes—standard or miniature. Both are members of the same breed.

Personality: The Dachshund is a popular pet that bonds closely with its owners. The breed isn't recommended for families with young children though. A Doxie may bite when it feels annoyed or threatened.

Country of Origin: Germany

Recognized by AKC: 1885

Training Notes: This breed is smart but stubborn. Owners may spend a lot of time training Doxies, especially with housetraining. Dachshunds respond well to positive rewards, such as praise or treats.

Care Notes: Dachshunds love to dig. For this reason owners must supervise their pets whenever they spend time outside. To avoid becoming overweight, Dachshunds should exercise regularly. Weekly brushing or combing is important for all coat types of this breed.

FUN FACT

Some people call Dachshunds hot dogs because of their length. But the food was actually named after the animal. Hot dogs were called dachshund sausages when they were first created.

English Foxhound

Appearance:
Height: 21 to 25 inches (53 to 64 cm)
Weight: 65 to 70 pounds (29 to 32 kg)

The English Foxhound has a short, tricolored coat. The hair is black, white, and tan and has a rough feel. This hard texture protects the dog from both harsh weather and low branches.

Personality: English Foxhounds are friendly, gentle dogs. Despite their loving nature, they aren't usually kept as pets. These dogs are meant for people who will take them hunting often. They are happiest when working as part of a pack of English Foxhounds in the field.

Breed Background: The English Foxhound is one of the few dog breeds that continues to be bred for its original purpose—hunting.

Country of Origin: United Kingdom

Recognized by AKC: 1909

Training Notes: As pack animals, these dogs learn many hunting techniques from watching their fellow English Foxhounds. Training English Foxhounds requires patience and understanding. They respond well to loving but firm leadership.

Care Notes: Daily exercise is ideal for this breed. An English Foxhound's short coat should be brushed regularly to keep it looking shiny.

FUN FACT
English Foxhounds were bred to run for miles at a time.

Greyhound

Appearance:

Height: 27 to 30 inches (69 to 76 cm)
Weight: 60 to 80 pounds (27 to 36 kg)

The Greyhound looks like it was built for speed. Its thin body and long legs make it the fastest dog in the AKC. This sighthound also has a long, thin head that gives it a wide field of vision. A Greyhound can see what is behind it without turning its head.

Personality: Greyhounds make ideal pets for active families. Despite their large size, these loving animals think they are lapdogs.

Breed Background: Greyhounds became popular in the United States during colonial times. Farmers used these dogs to chase wild rabbits away from their crops.

Country of Origin: Unknown; believed to be Egypt

Recognized by AKC: 1885

Training Notes: Greyhounds are easy to train but require patience. Early obedience training works well with Greyhounds.

Care Notes: Because of their tendency to run, Greyhounds need daily exercise in a large, fenced area. Their short coats do not require much grooming except occasional brushing and bathing.

FUN FACT

Greyhounds can reach 45 miles (72 km) per hour after running just 50 feet (15 m)!

FAMOUS DOGS

Harry Potter author J.K. Rowling adopted her Greyhound, Sapphire, from an animal shelter.

Ibizan Hound

Appearance:

Height: 22 to 29 inches (56 to 74 cm)
Weight: 42 to 55 pounds (19 to 25 kg)

The Ibizan Hound has two coat types: short-haired or wire-haired. The breed also comes in three colors, including red, white, or red and white. The dog's flesh-colored nose and eye rims give the breed a unique look.

FUN FACT

The Ibizan Hound's nickname is the Beezer.

Personality: Ibizan Hounds are affectionate and highly loyal to their human family members. These dogs take more time to warm up to strangers than many other breeds though.

Country of Origin: Egypt

Recognized by AKC: 1978

Training Notes: This breed learns quickly but becomes bored easily. Owners will have the best luck keeping training sessions short and fun. Early socialization training may also help Ibizans with warming up to new people.

Care Notes: Fenced yards give Ibizan Hounds the space to move that this breed needs. It is important that the fence is at least 6 feet (1.8 m) high. An Ibizan Hound can jump anything shorter. Its rough, short coat requires only occasional brushing and bathing.

Irish Wolfhound

Appearance:
Height: 28 to 38 inches (71 to 97 cm)
Weight: 110 to 125 pounds (50 to 57 kg)

FUN FACT

An Irish Wolfhound can measure 7 feet (2 m) tall when standing on its hind legs.

The Irish Wolfhound is the tallest of all dog breeds. Many people joke that this dog looks more like a horse than a dog. Horses definitely do not have this breed's rough and wiry coat, however. After its size, the breed is best known for its shaggy coat.

Personality: This huge breed needs plenty of space to run and play. An Irish Wolfhound is great with kids, but it should be supervised around small children because of its size.

Breed Background: The Irish Wolfhound is one of the oldest dogs still living today. It dates back to AD 391. The breed was developed to hunt elk, wild boars, and wolves.

Countries of Origin: Belgium, Ireland

Recognized by AKC: 1897

Training Notes: It is essential to begin training this breed when it is a puppy. Handling an **unruly** adult Irish Wolfhound is a challenging task for most people. If properly trained, Irish Wolfhounds will excel at dog sports, such as rally, agility, and lure coursing.

Care Notes: New owners of this breed should be prepared to buy lots of dog food. An adult Irish Wolfhound can eat 25 pounds (11 kg) of food in just one week. Despite its size an Irish Wolfhound doesn't need much exercise. Weekly brushing is important for these shaggy dogs.

Otterhound

Appearance:

Height: 24 to 26 inches (61 to 66 cm)
Weight: 66 to 115 pounds (30 to 52 kg)

The Otterhound's hair always looks messy. The thick, double coat comes in many different colors and combinations. The most common combination is black and tan.

FUN FACT

The Otterhound is considered one of the most endangered dog breeds worldwide. It is rarer than the Giant Panda.

Personality: Otterhounds are loving pets. They often play too rough for small children though. They are best suited for active families with older kids. Owners should take this dog along when going to the beach or lake whenever possible. Otterhounds greatly enjoy swimming.

Country of Origin:

United Kingdom

Recognized by AKC: 1909

Training Notes: Otterhound owners should make early socialization a top priority. Training may require patience, persistence, and positive rewards and praise.

Care Notes: This breed needs plenty of space for regular exercise. Weekly brushing is important to keep an Otterhound's hair clean and tangle-free.

Pharaoh Hound

Appearance:

Height: 21 to 25 inches (53 to 64 cm)
Weight: 45 to 55 pounds (20 to 25 kg)

The Pharaoh Hound's short coat, muscular body, and pointed ears make this breed easy to spot anywhere. Its coat ranges from tan to chestnut to red, with white markings on its chest, face, tail, and toes.

Personality: Owners of this breed call it clownish. Pharaoh Hounds love their human family members and are always entertaining them. These dogs aren't as friendly with new people, however. When a stranger arrives, a Pharaoh Hound can become **aloof**.

Breed Background: The Phraoh Hound looks a lot like dogs in Ancient Egyptian art. This is no accident, as the breed dates back to 3,000 BC in this part of the world.

Country of Origin: Egypt

Recognized by AKC: 1983

Training Notes: Pharaoh Hounds are highly intelligent and enjoy pleasing their owners. The breed can be stubborn, so training is important early on.

Care Notes: This breed feels cold easily. Dogs living in cooler climates should wear coats for time spent outdoors. These athletic dogs also need daily exercise. Their short coats need to be brushed every other week.

Plott

Appearance:

Height: 20 to 25 inches (51 to 64 cm)
Weight: 40 to 75 pounds (18 to 34 kg)

The Plott has a short, glossy coat. Its smooth hair is often brown with streaks of another color, called brindle. Some Plotts are also black with brindle.

FUN FACT

The Plott is the state dog of North Carolina.

Personality: Plotts are brave dogs that make loyal family pets. They can be cautious with strangers at first. Plotts warm up quickly once they see that a new person means no harm, however.

Breed Background: The Plott was named after a German immigrant, Johannes George Plott. He developed the Plott breed from hounds he brought with him to the United States more than 200 years ago.

Country of Origin: United States

Recognized by AKC: 2006

Training Notes: Plotts are smart animals that learn quickly. They need early and consistent training though. They will be overprotective of their toys and food unless they are trained to avoid these behaviors.

Care Notes: This breed needs a lot of exercise. Regular, weekly brushing or combing is recommended for Plotts in order to keep them looking their best.

Rhodesian Ridgeback

Appearance:
Height: 24 to 27 inches (61 to 69 cm)
Weight: 65 to 90 pounds (29 to 41 kg)

The Rhodesian Ridgeback is a large, muscular dog with a short coat. The breed is easy to identify by the ridge on its back. This long line is created by fur that grows in the opposite direction from the other hair in this area. The breed was named for this unusual feature.

FUN FACT

A Rhodesian Ridgeback can keep pace with a running horse for up to 30 miles (48 km).

Personality: Rhodesian Ridgebacks make great companions for families with older kids. Their high activity level makes them a perfect match for active people. This is a dog that wants to spend lots of time outdoors.

Breed Background: Also known as the African Lion Dog, this breed was developed to hunt large cats.

Area of Origin: Rhodesia (present-day Zimbabwe), southern Africa

Recognized by AKC: 1955

Training Notes: This smart breed is highly independent. Patient and consistent training works best with Rhodesians.

Care Notes: Rhodesian Ridgebacks are very athletic and need at least an hour of exercise each day. Because they have short coats, Rhodesians shed very little and require only weekly brushing.

Saluki

Appearance:

Height: 23 to 28 inches (58 to 71 cm)
Weight: 31 to 55 pounds (14 to 25 kg)

The Saluki looks a lot like a long-haired Greyhound. It has a long, thin body that helps it move quickly. These dogs are lean but incredibly muscular. Their feathery coats come in a variety of colors, including white, cream, red, tricolor, or black and tan.

FUN FACT

The Saluki is the official mascot of Southern Illinois University.

Personality: Salukis can be shy and take their time warming up to people. These dogs are suited for active families who will take the time to challenge them both physically and mentally.

Breed Background: Royal Ancient Egyptians turned their Salukis into mummies when the dogs died.

Country of Origin: Egypt

Recognized by AKC: 1929

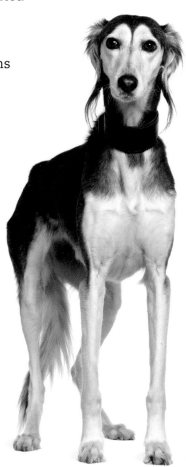

Training Notes: This breed is often described as cat-like. The Saluki's aloof nature can make training difficult. Patience and consistency are important, as well as early obedience training.

Care Notes: One of the best ways to provide this breed with the exercise it needs is to take it jogging. Salukis can keep up with even the most athletic human runners. These dogs don't shed a lot, but they should still be brushed weekly and bathed occasionally.

Scottish Deerhound

Appearance:
Height: 28 to 32 inches (71 to 81 cm)
Weight: 75 to 110 pounds (34 to 50 kg)

The Scottish Deerhound's coat is thick and wiry. Most dogs are dark blue-gray, although the breed comes in a variety of other colors too.

Personality: These friendly, athletic dogs can make great family pets as long as they get their exercise. The only thing a Scottish Deerhound enjoys more than going for a long walk is resting afterwards.

Country of Origin: Scotland

Recognized by AKC: 1886

Training Notes: This breed can be difficult to train. Scottish Deerhounds delight in their owners' praise, but Scotties prefer doing what they like. Early socialization and obedience training may help with this issue.

Care Notes: Exercise is very important for Scottish Deerhounds. They need space to run on a daily basis. Scottish Deerhounds are shedders. Their coats need brushing about twice per week to remove dead hair.

Whippet

Appearance:

Height: 18 to 22 inches (46 to 56 cm)
Weight: 20 to 40 pounds (9 to 18 kg)

Whippets are medium-sized sighthounds with great speed and balance. These short-haired dogs come in a variety of colors and markings, including black, blue, cream, red, and white.

Personality: Named for their whip-like speed, these dogs are surprisingly calm when they aren't playing. They enjoy napping on the floor or sofa. Some dogs will even snuggle with their favorite human family member.

Country of Origin: England

Recognized by AKC: 1888

Training Notes: Whippets are smart but sensitive. They need positive, gentle training. They respond well to praise and other rewards.

Care Notes: These athletic dogs excel at canine sports, such as agility and lure coursing. Without an organized activity, Whippets need a large amount of daily exercise. Their short coats should also be brushed weekly and bathed occasionally.

FUN FACT

Whippets are especially good at seeing in the dark.

Other Herding Breeds

Cirneco dell'Etna ▶

Known for: high endurance
Country of Origin: Italy
Recognized by AKC: 2015

....

Harrier

Known for: being talented hunters
and friendly pets
Country of Origin: United Kingdom
Recognized by AKC: 1885

....

Norwegian Elkhound

Known for: hunting
Country of Origin: Norway
Recognized by AKC: 1913

....

Petit Basset Griffon Vendeen

Known for: its nickname—the PBGV
Country of Origin: France
Recognized by AKC: 1990

Portuguese Podengo Pequeno

Known for: protectiveness
Country of Origin: Portugal
Recognized by AKC: 2012

Redbone Coonhound

Known for: hunting raccoons
Country of Origin: United States
Recognized by AKC: 2009

Treeing Walker Coonhound ▶

Known for: chasing its prey
up trees
Country of Origin: United States
Recognized by AKC: 2012

Glossary

aggressive (uh-GREH-siv)—strong and forceful

agility (uh-GI-luh-tee)—the ability to move fast and easily

aloof (uh-LOOF)—distant or not friendly

curry (KUR-ee)—to groom with a rubber or plastic, circular comb

mat (MAT)—a thick, tangled mass of hair

muzzle (MUHZ-uhl)—an animal's nose, mouth, and jaws

obedience (oh-BEE-dee-uhns)—obeying rules and commands

obese (oh-BEESS)—very fat

persistent (pur-SIST-uhnt)—continually trying to do something

saddle (SAD-uhl)—a colored marking on the back of an animal

socialize (SOH-shuh-lize)—to train to get along with people and other dogs

tick (TIK)—a small contrasting spot of color on the coat of a mammal

tricolor (TRYE-kuhl-er)—having three colors

unruly (uhn-ROO-lee)—hard to control or discipline

Read More

Finne, Stephanie. *Beagles*. Checkerboard Animal Library. Minneapolis, Minn.: ABDO Publishing, 2015.

Frischmann, Carol. *Dachshund*. Animal Planet: Dogs 101. Neptune City, N.J.: T.F.H. Publications, Inc., 2015.

Guillain, Charlotte. *Dogs*. Animal Abilities. Chicago: Raintree, 2013.

Internet Sites

FactHound offers a safe, fun way to find Internet sites related to this book. All of the sites on FactHound have been researched by our staff.

Here's all you do:

Visit *www.facthound.com*

Type in this code: 9781515703020

Check out projects, games and lots more at
www.capstonekids.com

Index